AMBITION & SUCCESS

ORISON SWETT MARDEN

ISBN: 978-93-95229-56-2
eISBN: 978-93-95229-57-9

Publisher: Pharos Books (P) Ltd.
Plot No.-55, Main Mother Dairy Road
Pandav Nagar, East Delhi-110092
Phone: 011-40395855, +14049995474
WhatsApp: +91 8368220032
E-mail: sales@pharosbooks.in
Website: www.pharosbooks.in
First Edition: 2023

AMBITION AND SUCCESS
ORISON SWETT MARDEN

Contents.

CHAPTER I
WHAT IS AMBITION?

"Ambition is the spur that makes man struggle with destiny: it is heaven's own incentive to make purpose great, and achievement greater."

In a factory where mariners' compasses are made, the needles, before they are magnetized, will lie in any position, wherever they are placed, but from the moment they have been touched by the mighty magnet and have been electrified, they are never again the same. They have taken on a mysterious power and are new creatures. Before they are magnetized, they do not answer the call of the North Star, the magnetic pole does not have any effect upon them, but the moment they have been magnetized they swing to the magnetic north, and are ever after loyal and true to their affinity.

Multitudes of people, like an unmagnetized needle, lie motionless, unresponsive to any stimulus until they are touched by that mysterious force we call ambition.

Whence comes this overmastering impulse which pushes human beings on, each to his individual goal? Where is the source of ambition, and how and when does it gain entrance into our lives?

How few of us ever stop to think what ambition really means, its cause, or significance! Yet, if we could explain just what ambition is, we could explain the mystery of the universe. The instinctive impulse to keep pushing on and up is the most curious and the most interesting thing in human life. It exists in every normal human being, and is just as pronounced and as real as the instinct of self-preservation.

I believe this incessant inward prompting, call it ambition or what we will, this something which pushes men to their goal, is the expression in man of the universal force of evolution which is flowing Godward, that it is a part of the great cosmic plan of creation. We do not create this urge, we do not manufacture it. Every normal person feels this imperious must which is back of the flesh, but not of it, this internal urge which is ever pushing us on, even at the cost of our discomfort and sacrifice.

It is a part of every atom, for all atoms are alive, and this upward impulse is in every one of them. It is in the instinct of the bee, the ant, and in all forms of insect and animal life.

The same kind of urge that is in the seed buried out of sight and which is ever pushing it up and out through the soil, prodding it to develop itself to the utmost and to give its beauty and fragrance to the world, is in each one of us. It is ever pushing us, urging us on to fuller and completer expression, to a larger, more beautiful life.

But for this desire to get on and get up, this God-urge, everything, even the universe itself, would collapse. Inertia would bring everything to a standstill.

If we obey this call we expand, blossom into beauty and develop into fruitage, but if we neglect or dissipate it, if we only half obey it, we remain mere scrub plants, without flower or fruitage.

That mysterious urge within us never allows us to rest but is always prodding us for our good, because there is no limit to human growth there is no satisfying human ambition—man's higher aspiration. When we reach the height which looks so attractive from below, we find our new position as unsatisfying as the old, and a perpetual call to go higher still rings in our ears. A divine impulse constantly urges us to reach our highest ideal.

"Faith and the ideal still remain the most powerful levers of progress and of happiness," says Jean Finot.

"Did you ever hear of a man who had striven all his life faithfully and singly toward an object," asked Thoreau, "and in no measure obtained it? If a man constantly aspires, is he not elevated? Did ever a man try heroism, magnanimity, truth, sincerity, and find that there was no advantage in them,—that it was a vain endeavor?"

Aspiration finally becomes inspiration and ennobles the whole life.

When the general habit of always aspiring, moving upwards and climbing to something higher and better is formed, all the undesirable qualities and the vicious habits will fade away; they will die from lack of nourishment. Only those things grow in our nature which are fed. The quickest way to kill them is to cut off their nourishment.

The craving for something higher and better is the best possible antidote or remedy for the lower tendencies which one wishes to get rid of.

Every faintest aspiration that springs up in our heart is a heavenly seed within us which will grow and develop into rich beauty if only it be fed, encouraged. The better things do not grow either in material or mental soil without care and nourishment. Only weeds, briers, and noxious plants thrive easily.

Most young people seem to think that ambition is a quality that is born in one and which cannot be materially changed, but the greatest ambition may be very materially injured in many different ways. The habit of procrastination, of postponing, the habit of picking out the easier tasks and putting off the difficult ones, for example, will very seriously impair the ambition. Whatever affects the ideals affects the ambition.

Ambition often begins very early to knock for recognition. If we do not heed its voice, if it gets no encouragement after appealing to us for years, it gradually ceases to trouble us, because, like any other unused quality or function, it deteriorates or disappears when unused.

God is whispering into the ear of all existence, of every created thing "Look up." Every sentient thing in the universe seems to be trying to get to a higher level. Everything is in the process of evolution, and the evolution is always upward. The butterfly does not become a grub. It is not the evolutionary law. The grub develops into a butterfly. It is never the other way.

Be careful how you discourage or refuse to heed that inner voice which commands you to go forward, for if you do it will become less and less insistent until finally it will cease to prod you, and when ambition is dead deterioration has set in.

That inner call to go forward, to push on to a higher good, is God's voice; heed it. It is your best friend and will lead you into light and joy.

***

CHAPTER II
THE SATISFIED MAN

F. W. ROBERTSON has said, "Whoever is satisfied with what he does has reached his culminating point—he will progress no more. Man's destiny is to be not dissatisfied, but forever unsatisfied."

One of the saddest things in life is to see men and women who started out with high hopes and proud ambitions settle down in mediocre positions, half satisfied just merely to get a living, to plod along indifferently.

Oh, what tragedy there is in being content with mediocrity, in getting into a state where one is indifferent to the larger, better things of life!

When you are satisfied with the life you are living, with the work you are doing, with the thought you are thinking, with the dreams you are dreaming, satisfied with the character you are building, with your ideals, you may be sure that you are already beginning to deteriorate.

There is little hope for the man who feels satisfied with himself, who does not know, "the noble discontent that stirs the acorn to become an oak." Man's ambition to improve something somewhere every day to get a little further on and a little higher up than he was the day before, an insatiable passion for bettering things all along the line, is the secret of human progress.

Do you realize, my young friend, that if the motive were big enough, if you had a very unusual incentive, you could materially improve upon what you now are satisfied to consider your best endeavor? As an employee you may think you are doing your level best, and are conscientious, loyal, true and industrious; and yet, if a great prize should be offered you to bring your work up to a certain higher standard for the next sixty days, would you rest until you had succeeded in very greatly improving what you now think is your best work?

Don't you think, you who pride yourself that it would be impossible to better what you are now doing, that if your name were over the door as proprietor instead of the name of the company you work for you could jack yourself up about fifty per cent; that you would find some way of doing it? Don't you think you would be a little more ambitious, make a little better use of your time, that you would try to call out a little more ingenuity and effectiveness, a little more resourcefulness? Do you think you would jog along in the same half-hearted manner, thinking more of your salary than of your opportunity to absorb the secrets of your employer's success? Do you think you would stand by without protest and see the merchandise injured, or wasted, when you could stop it; or that you would be so careless or make so many blunders yourself? Don't you think the prize to be gained would make you take a little more interest in things than you do now; make you a little more alert, more eager for the success of the business?

It is a deplorable sight to see so many young men and young women apparently so satisfied with themselves, with what they are doing, that they have no great yearnings, no insatiable longing for something higher and better.

Multitudes of capable employees are satisfied to plod along in mediocrity instead of rising to the heights, where their ability would naturally carry them. I have a friend who has a much superior brain to the man he is working for, and yet for a great many years he has been on an ordinary salary. He has never married. He takes life in an easy-going way and whenever I have tried to encourage him to go into business for himself, to show him how much superior he is to the man he is working for, he always says, "Why should I exert myself more or take on greater business, responsibilities? I have nobody but myself to consider. I like to have a good time, and don't want to have the worry, the care and anxiety of running a business of my own, although I know perfectly well I could do it if I wanted to."

Of course, the higher up in the world a man gets the greater his responsibility, but think of the satisfaction which comes from the consciousness that he has made the most of his talents, that he has not buried any of them in a napkin, the satisfaction which comes from the feeling that he has made good, that he has delivered his message to the world and delivered it like a man, that he has fulfilled his mission, that he has made the most possible of the material and the opportunities given him. The feeling that he has no regrets, that he has done his level best more than compensates for any additional effort and greater responsibility.

We tend to become like our aspirations. If we constantly aspire and strive for something better and higher and nobler, we cannot help broadening and improving. The ambition that is dominant in the mind tends to work itself out in the life. If this ambition is sordid and low and animal, we shall develop these qualities, for our lives follow our ideals.

Civilization has made its greatest advancement under the stress of necessity, under the leadership of a great ambition to satisfy the heart's yearnings for better things. We do our best work while we are trying desperately to match our dreams with their reality.

The struggle of man to rise a little higher, to get into a little more comfortable position, to secure a little better education, a little better home, to gain a little more culture and refinement, to possess that power which comes from being in a position of broader and wider influence through the acquirement of property, is what has developed the character and the stamina of our highest types of manhood to-day. This upward life-trend gives others confidence in us.

When we have attained a little success, when we have gained a little public applause, how many of us think we can relax our efforts, and before we realize it our ambition has disappeared, our energy evaporated. A sort of lethargy comes over us and lulls us into inaction.

First successes, and especially early successes, to many act like an opiate. They are overcome with inertia which only an unsatisfied and determined ambition can overcome. It takes more grit and a stronger will to force ourselves to do our level best after we have demonstrated without doubt that we have the ability to do what we undertake, than it does to achieve the actual first success itself.

One of the greatest enemies to ambition is personal inertia, and it is one of the hardest things to overcome. The temptation to slide along the line of the least resistance, to get into a comfortable position and take one's ease, is so strong that many allow it to master them. The ambition is not persistent enough or strenuous enough to shame them out of their inertia, or prod them on to greater things. Mediocrity is often a premium upon laziness. The poet tells us,

"He who would climb the heights sublime,
Or breathe the purer air of life,
Must not expect to rest in ease,
But brace himself for toil or strife."

One of the most discouraging problems in the world is that of trying to help the ambitionless, the half-satisfied, those who have not discontent enough in their natures to push them on, initiative enough to begin things, and persistency enough to keep going.

If a young man is apparently satisfied to drift along in a humdrum way, half content with his accomplishments, undisturbed by the fact that he has used but a very small part of himself, a very small percentage of his real ability, that his energies are running to waste in all sorts of ways, you cannot do much with him. If he lacks ambition, life, energy and vigor—is willing to slide along the line of the least resistance and exerts himself as little as possible, there is nothing upon which to build.

It is the young man who is not satisfied with what he does, and who is determined to better his best every day, who struggles to express the ideal, to make the possible in him a reality, that wins.

Activity is the law of growth; effort the only means of improvement. Whenever men have obeyed their lower nature and ceased to struggle to better their condition, they have deteriorated physically, mentally and morally; while, just in proportion as they have striven honestly and insistently to improve their situation, they have developed a larger and nobler human type.

When a man who is said to be the highest salaried official in the United States was asked to give the secret of his success, he replied, "I haven't succeeded. No real man ever succeeds. There is always a larger goal ahead."

It is the small man who succeeds in his own estimation. Really great men never reach their goal, because they are constantly pushing their horizon out further and further, getting a broader vision, a larger outlook, and their ambition grows with their achievement.

If you are getting a fair salary in a mediocre position there is danger of hypnotizing yourself into the belief that there is no need to exert yourself very much to get up higher. There is danger of limiting your ambition so that you will be half content to remain a perpetual clerk when you have the ability to do much better.

This satisfaction with the lesser when the greater is possible often results from relatives or friends telling you that you are doing well, and that you would better let well enough alone. These advisers say: "Don't take chances with a certainty. It is true you are not getting a very big salary, but it is a sure thing, and if you give it up with the hope of something better you may do worse." Don't let any one or any conditions make you think you have not the ability to match your longings. Wrapped up in every human being there are energies which, if unfolded, concentrated, and given proper attention will develop his highest ideal.

Our longings are creative principles, prophecies, indicative of potencies equal to the task of actual achievement. These latent potencies are not given to mock us. There are no sealed orders wrapped within the brain without the accompanying ability to execute them.

When you once get a glimpse of yourself as you were intended by your Maker to be, with all of your latent possibilities developed into realities; when you once see yourself as the superb man it is possible for you to be, nothing and no one but yourself can prevent you from attaining your ambition.

It is only the man who has stopped growing that feels satisfied with his achievements. The growing man feels a great lack of wholeness, of completeness. Everything in him seems to be unfinished because it is growing. The expanding man is always dissatisfied with his accomplishment, is always reaching out for something larger, fuller, completer.

***

CHAPTER III
THE INFLUENCE OF ENVIRONMENT

Environment has a great deal to do with man's ambition and achievement. It may make all the difference to you, my friend, between success and mediocrity, whether you are in a favorable environment and keep close to people who inspire and encourage you, who communicate to you the enthusiasm of their example, or whether you are surrounded by discordant conditions, and associate with people who have an opposite effect upon you.

We cannot associate with a really ambitious person without catching his spirit to a greater or less extent. We unconsciously reflect the people with whom we mingle much. Their mark is left upon us. We may not be able to see it ourselves, but other people can detect it.

Our Indian schools sometimes publish, side by side, photographs of the Indian youths as they come from the reservation and as they look when they are graduated—well dressed, intelligent, with the fire of ambition in their eyes. We predict great things for them; but the majority of those who go back to their tribes after struggling awhile to keep up their new standard gradually drop back to their old manner of living. There are, of course, many notable exceptions, but these are unusually strong characters, able to resist the downward-dragging tendencies about them.

If you interview the great army of failures, you will find that multitudes in it have failed because they never got into a stimulating, encouraging environment, because their ambition was never aroused, or because they were not strong enough to rally under depressing, discouraging, or vicious surroundings.

How often we see men and women with splendid brain power, with robust physiqúe, apparently superbly equipped for great careers, and yet they are living very ordinary lives, plodding along perhaps in mediocrity! This may be because they have never been aroused, and are totally ignorant of their powers. They may never have looked into the mirror of others who were succeeding along their lines and caught a glimpse of their own possibilities.

Whatever you do in life, make any sacrifice necessary to keep in an ambition-arousing atmosphere, an environment that will stimulate you to self-development. Keep close to people who understand you, who believe in you, who will help you to discover yourself and encourage you to make the most of your life. Choose companions and friends who are in sympathy with your ambition and who will give you their moral support and make you do what you are capable of doing. A few such friends may make all the difference to you between a grand success and a mediocre existence. We are all diamonds in the rough. Our environment may grind one, two or twenty facets. Some people never come in contact with the wheel which grinds a facet and lets in the light to reveal the hidden wonders. Many are buried as rough diamonds even though there may have been locked up in them great brilliancy and enormous value. Comparatively few human diamonds are ever so completely ground that all the hidden treasures are revealed.

Yet how trifling are the things which sometimes reveal the man! It may be the sight of a motto, the hearing of a sermon, a speech, the reading of some inspiring life history or some stirring ambition-arousing book, the encouraging conversation of a friend, of some one who believes in us and sees in us something which we never knew was there.

I know men who had apparently lost their ambition, who had been literally down and out, but who, by the reading of an inspiring book, or listening to a stimulating sermon, were thoroughly aroused to their possibilities even in a most discouraging environment and so completely transformed in a few months that they did not seem like the same individuals.

The speeches of Wendell Phillips, Webster, and Henry Clay, started a fire in many an ambitious youth which never went out, but which became a beacon light in American history.

We all know that the old-fashioned debating societies and clubs woke up the ambition of many a youth in the early days of our country, who might never have been heard from outside of his own little community but for the arousing influence of these debates.

The ambition of the boy who has lived on a farm in the back country is often aroused for the first time when he goes to the city. To him the metropolis is a colossal world's fair, where everybody's achievement is on exhibition. The progressive spirit which pervades the city is like an electric shock to him and arouses all of his latent energies, calls out his reserves. Everything he sees seems to be a summons to him to go forward, to push on.

He is constantly reminded by his city environment of what others have done. He sees the tremendous engineering feats, great factories and offices, vast businesses, all huge advertisers of man's achievement, and is stirred by an ambition to do something great himself.

Ambition is contagious. When a man meets others at the restaurant or club, or in other social ways, and hears accounts of their great successes, greater achievement, he immediately says to himself, "Why can't I do it?" "Why don't I do it?" and if he is of any account he probably says, "I will do it!" Then he goes back to his business with a new determination, perhaps with new ideas and new conceptions of the possibilities of his own success.

I have known young business men in the country who have not been specially successful who got tremendous impetus to their ambition by visiting larger city concerns in the same line of business. The greater successes touched their pride and they went back home and began to brace up and build up.

The same thing is true in professional life. The young country doctor visits a city hospital, attends clinics, sees operations by noted surgeons, and he goes home with his ambition fired and makes a vigorous resolution to try harder to be somebody in his own profession.

Men who are in business in small towns where they have no competition, and where they very seldom come in contact with those who are successful in their line of trade, are in constant danger of getting into a rut. Their ambition unconsciously becomes dulled, the energy oozes out of their efforts, and they take things easier, jog along in the same old manner year after year, and before they realize it dry rot gets into their business.

It is much easier to keep up one's interest and enthusiasm to do things worth while when we are right in touch with the ambitious, with those who are forging ahead with all their might, and who are perhaps working under great difficulties.

One of the unfortunate things about small towns and country places is the lack of stimulus to ambition. Many people living in remote country districts do not come in contact with standards by which they can measure and compare their own powers. They live a quiet uneventful life, and there is little in their environment to arouse the faculties which are not active in their vocation.

If you are ambitious to get on you will learn some splendid lessons from studying the qualities of those who have succeeded along the line of your ambition. You will find that it is a characteristic of the winner, that he is always thinking upon his life theme, is always headed towards the goal of his ambition, always planning along the line of his dreams. He talks the things, acts in the same direction, his whole life is absorbed in his theme. He radiates law, medicine, engineering, or manufacturing. By keeping his mind in a positive, creative condition he is constantly encouraging his mental magnet to attract the thing he is studying. If he is studying law he thinks law, pictures himself pleading at court, or giving advice in his office. He becomes a law magnet to attract law.

I know a man who says he will not take chances of the demoralization and the deterioration which would be worked in his nature by associating with habitual failures. He will have nothing to do with such people. He avoids doing business with them, for he says he finds that no matter how he may protest against it, he is unconsciously influenced by them.

There is no denying that there is much truth in this. We are unconsciously affected by the atmosphere surrounding us. Like attracts like. Successful people attract successful people. Failure attracts failure. Unlucky people attract unlucky people. Slovenly, slipshod people attract others of the same sort. "Birds of a feather flock together." The failures get together; the successes come together naturally.

On every hand we see young men who started out with brilliant prospects when they left college. Their friends predicted great things for them, but somehow or other, the enthusiasm of their school or college days soon oozed out. The continual suggestion of possibility which came to them from their school environment, the contagion from the ambitious spirit all about them, seemed then to multiply their prospects, to magnify their ability and to stir up their ambition until they really thought they were going to amount to something in the world, were going to accomplish something; but after they got away from the battery-charging institutions, they gradually lost their enthusiasm; their ambition dwindled. Their ideals changed with their environment. Little by little their dreams faded, and they resigned themselves to mediocrity or hopeless failure.

There is no environment so unfavorable, so discouraging, no situation so disheartening that a youth who is made of the right kind of material cannot change it. Lincoln, Benjamin Franklin, Fred Douglas, John Wanamaker, Marshall Field and thousands of other American boys found themselves in the midst of the most disheartening environment but made a new environment for themselves. It is possible for you to do the same.

The great trouble with most of us is that we never get aroused, never discover ourselves until late in life,—often too late to make much out of the remnant that is left. It is very important that we become aroused to our possibilities when young, thus we may overcome the most unfavorable environment and get the greatest possible efficiency out of our lives.

***

CHAPTER IV
UNWORTHY AMBITIONS

There are scores of people in our great cities who do not really live at all. They merely exist. They are the slaves of a morbid ambition and a greed that has grown to be a monster. Many of these people take very little comfort; they are always on a strain to keep up appearances, to maintain homes in portions of the city where they can ill afford to live, to keep automobiles when they can barely afford a bicycle, to wear clothing and jewelry which is beyond their means, and they keep themselves constantly worried over it, killing their legitimate comfort and enjoyment through the exhaustion of the strain and stress,—and all for nothing that is real or permanent, nothing that adds to their character or well being.

Such people have a perfect mania for trying to make other people think they are better off than they really are, that they amount to more than they really do, that they cut a bigger figure in the world than is actually the case. In other words, they make themselves pitiable slaves of other people's eyes. They go through life not doing the things they ought to do, what is best for their welfare and growth. Their lives are superficial because they do not live in or deal in realities. Everything about them is deceiving. They live masked lives. Few people know them as they really are. They only know them as they pretend to be. What do these people, who are always chasing shadows, get out of life, anyway?

There is an ambition which reminds one of a bird whose voracious appetite can never be satisfied. It grows on what it feeds, and the more it eats, the more ravenous the appetite. Woe be it to him who caters to a false ambition! He follows it blindly, expects that it will give him peace when it is satisfied, but alas, it is never satisfied. It is like the water in the enchanted story: the more the victim drank of it, the greater was his burning thirst. Such an ambition is fatal, and will surely wreck him who blindly pursues it. It will ruin his health and will rob him of all that is dearest and sweetest in life.

There are a great many people in this country who are committing suicide upon many years of their lives by being slaves of an inordinate ambition.

One of the most pathetic phases of our civilization is that men and women in poor health, devitalized from over-work, are goaded on way beyond their strength by a fiendish ambition. Their pride and their vanity say to them, "Now, it will not do to slow down. We must keep up the pace with our neighbors. People who do not keep up appearances in these days are nobodies. We must keep going, no matter how we feel. We must make more money, we must show more evidence of our prosperity. We must put up a better front or Mrs. Grundy will pass the suspicion along that we are, after all, not much of a success, that we lacked the ability to do what people thought we were going to do. No matter how we feel we must keep up, keep pushing, keep going, crowd on more steam, take stimulants and drugs, if necessary, goad ourselves on. It is absolutely imperative to keep pushing."

Oh, what fools pride and vanity make of us, especially when we are in no condition to keep up the pace, when we owe it to ourselves to slow down, when it is positively wicked to crowd on more steam! How many people are driven into the grave by the lash of a mortgage on a farm, on a home, or on their business, put there in an attempt to satisfy some over-vaunting ambition!

Debt has made more people miserable, ruined the peace of mind of more human beings, the comfort and the happiness of more homes, than almost anything else in the universe. It is a terrible thing to so mortgage oneself to others that we must make slaves of ourselves. How much better to live simply, to struggle on in poverty until we can improve our position than to compromise ourselves with debt, sell ourselves to a mortgage, or a bill of goods!

What an easy thing it is to borrow money, to give a note or to give a mortgage! We believe at the time that we can pay all right, but no one can be certain that things will go all right with him. No one knows what the times may bring forth. No one knows whether his health and strength will be spared, or how soon he may be physically or mentally disabled.

The only true measure of real success is the quality of the ambition. If the animal figures too largely in your ambition, if the quality is coarse, the success will be cheap, no matter how great the quantity.

It is an unfortunate thing that so many of our youth should start out in life with only one aim; and that is to make money. This becomes the leading purpose in their lives and warps their way of looking at things. Everything else is seen in dwarfed proportions. They do not consider making a life, building character; they are bent only on making money. This is the all-absorbing topic everywhere.

The goal we hold in the mind is the model which shapes our lives, and its character is reflected in everything we do. Think, therefore, what the influence must be of pointing all our faculties, focusing all of our energies upon the money-making goal! How it must warp and twist and wrench out of their natural orbit the more delicate sentiments, the finer faculties. When everything in us looks moneyward, and the gaze is held persistently upon the dollar and what it will bring, what must be the havoc, the tragedy, the fatal damage in the affections, the friendships, and the social faculties! When the affections are chilled and the friendships strangled what is there left in a man but the monster, brute qualities?

This is why a youth who starts out with noble aspirations, with fine sensibilities and responsive affections, often becomes hardened in his business career. His finer sensibilities and more delicate faculties atrophy from disuse, because he overdevelops the grasping, greedy, selfish faculties by the modern mania for the almighty dollar.

The transformation is so insidious that he does not half realize it until he finds himself stooping to scheming and plotting and underhand cunning, which would have shocked him a few years earlier.

When a man once gets in the power of the selfish, greedy, grasping monster within him, which he has fed and catered to so long that it has become a giant, it is almost impossible to wrench himself away, and he often becomes the slave of the very thing he once despised and loathed.

It is always a question of what is uppermost in the ambition, the dominant aim, that shapes the life most. When a man has pursued an aim for years which tends to dry up the best within him, when he has used all of his life forces, all of his energies, to feed that unworthy ambition until it has become a monster which controls him, he is a pitiable creature. There is no more distressing sight in the world than that of one who is completely in the clutches of a heartless, grasping, greed. Spurred on by the morbid ambition which has taken possession of him, he is madly pursuing the dollar which haunts him, until he is deaf to all appeals of his finer self, and has lost all taste for that which he once enjoyed.

Multitudes of people seem to think that if they were only in an ideal environment, where they would be free from worry or anxiety regarding the living-getting problem, if they were free from pain and in vigorous health, they would be perfectly happy. As a matter of fact, we are not half so dependent for happiness upon our environment, or upon circumstances, as we sometimes imagine we are. False ambition, envy and jealousy are responsible for much of our uneasiness, our restlessness and discontent. Our minds are so intent upon what other people have and are doing that we do not get a tithe of the enjoyment and satisfaction out of our own work, out of our own possessions, that they should afford us.

An inordinate ambition, a desire to get ahead of others, a mania to keep up appearances at all hazards, whether we can afford it or not, all these things feed selfishness, that corrosive acid which eats away our possible enjoyment and destroys the very sources of happiness. The devouring ambition to get ahead of others in money making, to outshine others socially, develops a sordid, grasping disposition which is the bane of happiness. No man with greed developed big within him need expect to be happy. Neither contentment, satisfaction, serenity, affection, nor any other member of the happiness family can exist in the presence of greed, or an inordinate, selfish ambition.

We have had some conspicuous examples of political aspirants who have put their personal ambition above their duty to their party and their country. Time and again one or the other of the great political parties has been well-nigh ruined by a man who could put his own personal ambition against even his country's welfare.

It is a dangerous thing to put personal ambition above duty, anyway, but especially so to a politician or statesman, who is rendered doubly dangerous if he possesses great magnetic qualities.

We do not always know where the following of ambition's call will lead us, but we do know this, that by being loyal to ambition and doing our best to follow it in its normal, wholesome state, when not perverted by selfishness, by love of ease or self-gratification, it will lead to our best and highest welfare, that when we follow, when we put ourselves in a position to give it the best and the freest scope, it will lead us to the highest self-expression of which we are capable, and will give us the greatest satisfaction. We know, too, that when our ambition is perverted to base ends our lives go all awry; when we are false to the higher voice within us, we are discontented, unhappy, inefficient, and our lives are ineffective.

When a man becomes so infatuated with the mania for wealth, position, fame or notoriety that he focuses his whole soul, all his powers and energies, upon a false ideal,—upon a selfish, narrow goal, he develops only a very small part of himself and he becomes very narrow. He lives most who lives truest. He lives most who touches life in the largest number of the largest and highest points.

Don't start out in life with a false standard; a truly great man makes official position and money and houses and estates look so mean and poor that we feel like sinking out of sight with our cheap laurels and our ill-earned gold.

***

CHAPTER V
AMBITION KNOWS NO AGE LIMIT

What has become of that something which in your youth keyed your determination up to such a lofty pitch? What has become of that something in you which would not let you rest, which robbed you of sleep, which constantly prodded you, bombarded you with visions of the great and wonderful things you were going to do in the future?

One of the earmarks of old age is the cooling down of the fires of ambition. While they burn brightly, as long as you feel just as eager and as determined as in your younger days to do your level best, to get up and to get on in the world, to keep growing, to keep improving, you are not aging very much. Your years may dispute this, but as long as a man aspires, as long as he is eager to grow, as long as he yearns and struggles to better his best he is not old.

When we are getting along in years there is always a great temptation to make ourselves believe that we have a right to let up a bit and to take things easier, to get rid of as much drudgery as possible. We have less and less inclination for the strenuous struggle to attain that which characterized our youth. The great danger at this time is that as we let up a bit in our efforts our ambition will decline, all of our life standards drop.

Many people are not quite as painstaking, not quite as particular when they get along in years as in their younger days. It is so much easier then to slide along easily, not to trouble about one's dress and personal appearance, to hypnotize oneself into thinking, "Well, it does not matter very much now, I am no longer young."

One of the most difficult things one is called upon to do as the years pass is to keep his ambition from dying, his ideals clear and clean-cut, his interest in his work from getting stale.

The secret of keeping the ambition fresh and bright is in keeping up the interest. The artist who is in love with his work, no matter how old, never loses his zest, his enthusiasm. He goes to his canvas in old age with all the interest and eagerness of his youth.

Many men and women age through sheer laziness, mental inertia, indifference. They are only half alive. They are not willing to take the trouble to pay the price for perpetual youth, to keep their ambition from lagging.

Some people seem to think that the ambition to do a certain thing in life is a permanent quality which will remain with them. It is not. One of the first symptoms of age and deterioration in one's work is the gradual, unconscious oozing out, shrinkage, of one's ambition. There is no one quality in our lives that requires more careful watching and constant bracing up, jacking up, so to speak, than our ambition, especially when we are advancing in years, and do not keep in an atmosphere which tends to arouse one to life's possibilities. Without realizing it, or meaning to, we then easily become victims of the human inclination to take things easy, not to exert oneself very much.

No matter how high our youthful ambition, it is very easy to let it wane with the years, to allow our standards to drop. The moment we cease to brace ourselves up, to watch ourselves, we begin to deteriorate, just as a child does when his mother ceases to pay strict attention to him and lets him have his own way. The tendency of the majority at every age of existence is to go along the line of least resistance, to take the easiest way. The race instinct to climb is continually at war with the lower nature which would drag it down. Even the noblest beings are not free from the struggle of the higher with the lower which goes on ceaselessly throughout nature. It is the triumph over the lower that keeps the race on the ascent.

There is no more pitiable sight in the world than that of a person in whom ambition is dead,—a man who has repeatedly denied that inward voice which bids him up and on, a man in whom ambition's fires have gone out from the lack of fuel. There is always hope for a person, no matter how bad he may be, as long as his ambition is alive; but when that has disappeared, the great life-spur, the impelling motive is gone.

It requires a great deal and a great variety of food to keep the ambition vigorous. Unless it is well fortified it does not amount to anything. It must be backed by a robust will power, stern resolve, physical energy, and great powers of endurance, to be effective.

The habit of watching the ambition constantly and keeping it alive, is absolutely imperative to those who would keep from deteriorating. Everything depends on the ambition.

If we lived and thought more scientifically there would not be such a dropping of standards, such a dulling of ideals, and letting down in our efforts with advancing years.

Whatever our ambition may be, nothing else can be quite so precious to most of us as life, and we want that life at its best. Every normal person dreads to see the mark of old age, the symptoms of decrepitude, and wants to remain fresh, buoyant, robust, as long as possible. Yet most people do not take sensible precautions to preserve their youth and vigor. They violate the health laws, longevity laws; sap their vitality in foolish, unnatural living, in deteriorating habits.

I have a friend who is always referring to his age. He has formed a habit of constantly dwelling upon his declining years, and keeping the picture of decrepitude in his mind. "You know, when a man gets past sixty he can't stand what he once could," he will say.

The idea that our energies and forces must begin to decline and the fires of ambition die out after a certain age is reached has a most pernicious influence upon the mind. We do not realize how impossible it is for us to go beyond our self-placed "dead-line" limits, to do what we really believe we cannot do.

No one is old until the interest in life is gone out of him, until his spirit becomes aged, until his heart becomes cold and unresponsive; as long as he touches life at many points he can not grow old in spirit. A man is old, no matter what his years, when he is out of touch with youth, with its ideals, its points of view, out of touch with the spirit of his times; when he has ceased to be progressive and up-to-date.

Many of the grandest characters that ever lived have retained their youthful mentality up to the very last of a long life. There was no deterioration in the mind of Marshall Field. When in his advanced years he never showed any inclination to take less pains, any cooling of ambition, any inclination to bank his fires, to drop his standards, to lower his ideals. We know that Gladstone's mind was right in its prime at eighty.

Many a man signs his death warrant when he retires from business. Retiring from business to many means practically retiring from life, that is, from real living, because they have nothing to retire to. They have not prepared themselves for retirement to anything outside of routine business life. They have lost most of their friends in their absorption in business and their exclusive mode of living. They have never developed their social faculties, their love of art, of music, or of reading. The whole life has gone into one business channel and when out of this they are lost.

Life means little without a purpose. Once his life aim is gone man simply exists—he does not really live. A high ideal, a lofty purpose, a noble aim, whatever tends to make man look up and struggle up, tends to improve his health condition and prolong the life. The soul that aspires, other things being equal, has the longest life. Aspiration is a perpetual tonic; it stimulates all the faculties.

***

CHAPTER VI
MAKE YOUR LIFE COUNT

Everywhere we see men and women doing the lower, the commoner things, seemingly satisfied to do them all their lives, when they have the ability to do the higher.

Many people do not start out with ambition enough to spur them to do big things. They make a large career practically impossible at the very outset, because they expect so little of themselves. They have a narrow, stingy view of life and of themselves which limits their ambition to a little, rutty, poverty-stricken groove.

If I could give the American youth but one word of advice, it would be that which Michael Angelo wrote under a diminutive figure on a canvas in Raphael's studio, when he called and found the great artist out, "Amplius," meaning "larger." Raphael needed no more. This word meant volumes to him. I advise every youth to frame this motto, hang it, up in his room, in his store, in his office, in the factory where he works, where it will stare him in the face. Constant contemplation of it will make his life broader and deeper.

A fine ambition is a splendid life steadier. It holds us to our task; keeps us from yielding to the hundred temptations that might ruin us.

What chaos there would be but for man's ambition to get up and get on in the world and to improve his condition.

Nothing so strengthens the mind and enlarges the horizon of manhood as a constant effort to measure up to a worthy ambition. It stretches the thought, as it were, to a larger measure, and touches the life to finer issues.

"I am determined to make my life count," said a poor young immigrant with whom I was talking not long ago. Now, there is a resolution that is worth while, because it is backed by a high ambition, the determined purpose to be a man, to make his life one of service to humanity.

This young fellow works hard during the day, studying in a night school, and improving himself in every possible way in his odds and ends of time.

This is the sort of dead-in-earnestness that wins. This is the sort of material that has made America distinctive among all the nations of the earth. This is the sort of determination that gave us a Lincoln, an Andrew Jackson, an Edison, a John Muir—all our great men, native born or adopted sons.

Could any one have a nobler ambition than this—to make his life count? One cannot imagine its failure, backed up by dead-in-earnestness.

The quality of the ambitions of a people at any time locates them in the scale of civilization. The ideals of an individual or a nation measure the actual condition and the future possibilities and probabilities.

The trouble with many youths is they start out with no definite plan, no one unwavering aim, for success, no worth while goal in view. They just look for a job. It may fit them or it may not, and they plod along, doing their work indifferently, with no spirit or ambition to push them towards the heights.

© Underwood & Underwood

JOHN MUIR

It is astonishing how many people there are who have no definite aim or ambition, but just exist from one day to another with no well-defined life plan. Although the great world war has done much to bring our youth to a realization of their responsibilities and raised their ideals to a lofty height we still see all about us on the ocean of life young men and women aimlessly drifting without rudder or port, throwing away time, without serious purpose or method in anything they do. They simply drift with the tide. If you ask one of them what he is going to do, what his ambition is, he will tell you he does not exactly know yet what he will do. He is simply waiting for a chance to take up something.

"Between the great things that we cannot do and the small things we will not do, the danger is that we shall do nothing," says Adolphe Monod.

It is not enough for success to have ability, education, health. Hundreds of thousands have all these and still fail, or live in mediocrity, because they do not put themselves in an attitude or condition for achievement. Their ability is placed at a disadvantage by the lack of a big motive, the stimulus of a worthy ambition.

"The important things in life is to have a great aim and to possess the aptitude and perseverance to attain it," says Goethe.

Of course, many people are hindered in the race through no fault of their own, but the vast majority of those who cease to climb and give up (often right in sight of their goal), do so from some weakness or defect. Many of them lack continuity of purpose or persistency; others lack courage or determination. Many of these unfortunates would attain to at least something of real success by merely sticking to their tasks.

If the motive is big enough the ability to match it is usually forthcoming. There is not one of you, my friends, who could not be more alert, more original, more ingenious, more resourceful, more careful, more thorough, more level-headed; not one of you who could not use a little better judgment a little more forethought, a little more discrimination, if you saw a tempting prize ahead of you as a reward.

"Whatever may be your ambition, play fair with yourself. Quit the side issues." Cut out the diversions. Live with and for your big ambition. Drop all else to attain your end and you will win—you will be and you will have what you want.

"Take a lesson in pruning and lop off the useless branches which consume vitality and obscure the sunshine." That card club that interferes with early rising; that light reading that takes your mind off preparation for bigger things, and all other wasteful habits. Have you cut them off? If you have not it is because you don't want the "big thing" hard enough to deserve it, and you won't get it unless you prune off the useless habits that are diverting your energy and keeping you away from the main chance.

"Success in life is a process of selection and elimination—a choosing between the worthless and the worth while. To get time for things that count you must save time by eliminating all else. Copy the athlete at the training table, feed on that which builds you up and keeps you fit for the struggle."

Unless you are inspired by a great purpose, a resolute determination to make your life count, you will not make much of an impression upon the world about you. The difference in the quantity and quality of success is largely one of ambition and determination. If you lack these you must cultivate them vigorously, persistently, or you will be a nobody. I have never known any one to make a place for himself in the world, who did not keep his purpose alive by the constant struggle to reach his goal. The moment ambition sags, we lose the force that propels us; and once our propelling power is gone we drift with the tide of circumstances.

"The youth who does not look up will look down, and the spirit that does not soar is destined to grovel."

A young stenographer said to me once that if she felt sure she had the ability to become an expert literary stenographer, she would go to evening school and would study nights and holidays, and improve herself in every possible way; but if she was convinced that she could never attain very great speed, she would simply prepare herself for ordinary letter dictation, and let it go at that.

She did not seem to think that making the most possible of what ability she had would give her a correspondingly good position, or that the best possible training she could give herself would be the best possible investment she could make, and would give her infinite satisfaction.

The less ability you have, my young friend, the more important it is that you make the most possible out of it. If you are obliged to get your living, and, some of you, to support a family and make a home with one talent, you certainly need to make the most possible out of it, and to put forth much greater effort than if you had been given ten talents.

***

CHAPTER VII
VISUALIZE YOURSELF IN A BETTER POSITION

NO matter in what business you may be, or what your profession, your prime ambition should be to attain a high-water mark in it. The love of excellence is the lodestar that leads the world onward. It is this that makes not only the successful business or professional man, but also the all-round successful person in any line of endeavor.

Andrew Carnegie said, "I would not give a fig for the young man in business who does not already see himself a partner, or the head of the firm."

Do not rest for a moment in your thought of yourself as a head clerk, foreman, or manager in any concern, no matter how big it is. Say each day to yourself, "My place is higher up." Be king in your dreams. Vow that you will reach the position with untarnished reputation, and make no other vow to distract your attention.

I am frequently asked by youths and young men whether I think they really have enough in them to make much of a success in life, anything that will be distinctive or worth while, and I answer, "Yes, you have. I know you have the ability to succeed, but I don't know that you will. That rests entirely with you. If you have the energy and the will to succeed nothing can hold you back. But if you have not, no amount of education, no pull or influence, no power on earth outside of yourself can push or lead or boost you into success."

There is nothing so important in your life as your mental attitude towards yourself, what you think of yourself, the model which you hold of yourself and your possibilities. If this is small, narrow, and dwarfed your life will correspond.

You must see yourself above a clerkship or you will never be anything higher than a clerk. You must visualize yourself in a better position, and hold constantly a grim determination to reach it or you will never get there. Never for a moment blur your motive or weaken your determination by harboring a doubt of your ability to reach your goal. Whenever you do this you are neutralizing just so much of the force which would take you there.

Remember, there is a partnership waiting for you somewhere if you are big enough and determined enough and have pluck enough to take it. If you do not there is probably someone very near you who will do so, someone who perhaps has not had nearly as good an opportunity as you have had. And in the years to come, if you do not take advantage of this opportunity to climb, you will no doubt, grumble at your "ill luck" and wonder how Billy or Johnny or Jo, who worked alongside of you, managed to get the partnership or coveted position.

A recent writer says: "My advice to all those just starting to travel life's turnpike is: 'Don't start until you have your ideal. Then don't stop until you get it.'"

LINCOLN STUDYING BY THE FIRELIGHT.

Very few of us realize how dependent our growth is on some special stimulus. Every act must have a motive. We do nothing outside of our automatic habitual acts without an underlying motive. Perhaps the stronger life motive of the average man is that which comes from his desire to get up in the world.

There was a force behind Lincoln which drove him from a log cabin up to the White House. There was a vision of the North Pole which haunted Peary, filled him with ambition to climb to the earth's uttermost boundary, and finally drove him, after repeated failures, to the Pole. The same indomitable inner force urged the despised young Jew, Benjamin Disraeli, to push his way up through the lower classes in England, up through the middle classes, up through the upper classes, until he stood a master, self-poised, upon the topmost round of political and social power, the prime minister of the greatest country in the world.

The story of those men is the same at bottom as that of every man who has attained greatness. They were continually urged forward and upward by some inward prompting they could not resist.

This instinctive impulse to keep pushing on and up is the most curious and the most interesting thing in human life. It exists in every normal human being, and is just as pronounced and as real as the instinct of self-preservation. Upon this climbing instinct rests the destiny of the race. Without it men would still be savages, and living in caves and huts. Civilization, as we know it, would not exist. There would be no great cities, no great factories, no railroads, no steamships, no beautiful homes or parks, pictures, sculpture or books, but for this mysterious urge which we call ambition.

The best of every man's work is above and beyond himself, and is accomplished in the struggle to attain a lofty ideal. The artist stands aside and points through his work to a glimpse of the universal art. In his inspired moments the individuality of the orator is melted and fused into the all-pervading fire of eloquence. In art or business, in science or the daily commonplace tasks of life, the gods will move along toward the line of absolute excellence or they will leave us to our own devices.

We do our most effective work in our struggle to get what we are after, to arrive at the goal of our ambition. We put forth our greatest effort, our most strenuous endeavor, while we are climbing, not after we have arrived at our goal. This is one reason why rich men's sons rarely achieve any great personal success. They lack the climbing motive of necessity, that tremendous urge, the prodding of ambition which drives us on to achieve what we desire and are capable of attaining. Ambition is the leader of all great achievement. It is the forerunner which goes ahead and clears a way for the other faculties.

The ambition is not always a safe guide, however. There are two wings to genius. Common sense and good judgment must accompany the ambition, or it will very often run away with a man. We have seen splendid pieces of machinery, whose iron fingers would punch holes through solid steel plates without a single jar. The machinery accomplishes this wonderful feat because of a huge balance-wheel. It is the stored-up power, velocity, and momentum which enable it to accomplish this wonderful task. Take away the balance-wheel, and the machinery, which does its work as easily as a cook would make the holes in rolled-out pastry, falls all to pieces the moment the balance-wheel is removed. The balance-wheel is the secret. The judgment is man's balance-wheel—great common sense, horse sense. His ambition will run away with him if he does not have this.

The young man who overestimates his ability, who plunges beyond his depth, who is over-confident, whose self-trust is not based upon an accurate knowledge of his ability and limitations, almost always comes to grief. It is just as necessary to know what you are not qualified for, and to let it alone, as to know what you can do, and do it.

"Study yourself," says Longfellow, "and most of all, note well wherein kind nature meant you to excel."

It takes a giant to do a giant's work. What a Morgan or a Carnegie would do with perfect ease and safety, might be as impossible for you to accomplish as to lift yourself by your own boot straps. On the other hand, you may be able to do something which even a Morgan could not do. Study your own adaptations. Try to get a measure of your possibilities.

A man should early take an inventory of his ability and locate himself where he belongs. If he has but one talent he should not try to train with the ten-talent man. He should simply try to make the most of his one talent.

It is impossible to make one talent do the work of ten talents, no matter how ambitious, or how much energy one may fling into his work.

A great brain does a great thing easily. We all do our best work without overstraining. It is dangerous to over-tax one's faculties.

I have seen a college student who has overstrained his brain until he has seriously marred his mental power in the foolish effort to try to head his class when he was not a natural scholar. He seemed to think that by making a superhuman effort, studying all the time when others were at play, during holidays and Sundays, always plugging, plugging, plugging,—he could overcome any handicap. While he managed to come pretty near leading his class he never completely rallied from the effects of overstraining his brain.

It is a great thing to be able to measure our talents, to understand ourselves so thoroughly that we will undertake just so much as we are able to accomplish, and will not aim at the unattainable.

***

CHAPTER VIII
THWARTED AMBITION

ALL about us we see people who seem to have no special zest in life, no great enthusiasm for anything; there is a great disappointment somewhere in their lives. Why are they so unhappy?

No one loses his interest in life, or becomes indifferent to his work unless he has been thwarted in the carrying out of his ambition, or for some other reason has been unable to find his right place in life. Wherever we see discontent, unhappiness, unrest, we may be sure that the person exhibiting these conditions is a round peg in a square hole, or has not been able to realize his dreams. For some reason his heart has been cheated of its ideal. A thwarted ambition seems to wrench the whole nature out of its normal orbit.

There is no suffering, except remorse, so fatal as that which comes from the consciousness of blasted hope, stifled aspiration. To be conscious that one possesses decided ability for some particular calling, and to be compelled by circumstances, year after year, to be chained to drudgery which the heart loathes, requires supreme courage. To feel that there is no probability, or even possibility, of ever being able to express that great hungry longing, pent up in the heart, filling it almost to bursting, to drag through the weary years trying to be cheerful and hopeful and helpful to those one loves and yet to feel that his devotion to them has made the other thing impossible to him, to suffer in silence disappointment which makes the heart sick, is the greatest test of real manhood or womanhood.

It is very easy to criticize other people who have not risen in the world, as perhaps we have; but they may be heroes compared with us. We can never tell what tragedies may be going on in their hearts, or from what tortures of disappointed ambition and blasted hopes they may be suffering. To be compelled to go through life without any possibility of satisfying the great soul hunger, of realizing the infinite longings of the heart, is torture. There is no compensation for this except from the sense of duty done to others who would have suffered had we tried to realize our ambition.

I know a beautiful woman, of charming personality, who has a great musical talent, a superb voice and yet, she scarcely dares mention the subject of music in the presence of her husband, who flies into a passion at the mere suggestion of her developing her wonderful talent.

All of her friends think it is criminal of her not to use her great gift but she feels forced to smother her ambition. Her husband, although well able to meet the expense will not consider her taking lessons or making any effort to improve this God-given talent. The result is a blight is setting on this woman's life.

She tries to be cheerful and to do her duty; but those who understand her can see the slow strangulation processes going on, which is undermining her ambition and destroying her health.

I recently heard through a piano dealer of another woman of great musical talent who with money bequeathed to her purchased a beautiful, longed-for piano. Her husband made life so unbearable to her because of it that she returned it to the makers, who, appreciating her position, generously returned to her the money paid them for it.

Is there anything more cruel than to strangle a talent which was intended to be a perpetual joy as well as to give us success? Is there anything more wicked than to murder a divine ambition, to destroy sacred aspirations; anything more cruel than to make a human being miserable who is intended to be happy, to rob one of all possibility of doing that which she was made to do? Yet there are thousands of husbands who are doing this, and they wonder why their wives are not always buoyant and bubbling over with vivacity and life, why they are not always cheerful, hopeful and resourceful.

Many husbands do not mean to be selfish in their home life, and really believe they are generous, but their minds are so focused upon themselves and their ambition that they can only think of a wife in reference to themselves. Whereas the highest love has the highest welfare of the individual at heart, not its own.

Ambition often blinds one to justice.

There is nothing more pitiable than to see a man the victim of an inordinate, selfish ambition to advance himself at all costs, to gain fame, or notoriety, or pleasure, no matter who is sacrificed in the process.

Many women have a marvelous way of hiding their griefs, covering up their disappointment; but such disappointment may mar the whole life.

There is something so utterly discouraging, disheartening, in being forced to give up the careers they long for, that the nature never entirely rallies from the shock. Everywhere we see these burned-out shells of individuals who have been robbed of their normal pursuit. They are ambitionless, restless, ineffective weaklings, mere pygmies of their possible selves.

Ella Wheeler Wilcox gives some wise advice that the dissatisfied and unhappy man or woman whose ambition has been thwarted may heed to advantage.

"Do not waste your vitality in hating your life; find something in it which is worth liking and enjoying, while you keep steadily at work to make it what you desire," she says. "Be happy over something every day, for the brain is a thing of habit, and you cannot teach it to be happy in a moment, if you allow it to be miserable for years."

There is a powerful tonic in holding the conviction that you are in the world for a purpose, that you are here to help, that you have a part to perform which no one else can take for you, because every one else has his own part to fill in the great life drama. If you do not act your role, there will be something lacking, a want in the production. No one ever amounts to much until he feels this pressure—that he was made to accomplish a certain thing in the world, to fill a definite part. Then life seems to take on a new meaning.

"Few of us," says Sir John Lubbock, "realize the wonderful privileges of living; the blessings we inherit, the glories and beauties of the Universe which are our own if we choose to have it so; the extent to which we can make ourselves what we wish to be; or the power we possess of securing peace, of triumphing over pain and sorrow."

We go through life with our eyes steadily fixed on some distant goal, straining every nerve to reach it. We pass on our way opportunities innumerable of helping others over rough places, of brightening and beautifying the commonplace life of every day. But we see them not.

Man was made for growth; to realize peace, poise, satisfaction.

An ambition to be a man, to stand for more in the community, to push our horizon farther and farther away from us, to think a little higher each day, to think a little more of ourselves, to have a little more faith in ourselves and in everybody else, an ambition to be of real use in the world is an ambition worthy of the man God created, and cannot but bring happiness to the individual.

In the white light of history, before the tribunal of justice, we shall not be judged for what we seem to be or have achieved, but for what we are and by what we have tried to do.

In the judgment of this tribunal, from which there is no appeal, many failures will be approved as successes, and many successes will be adjudged failures.

It will be easy to find the story of some boy who remained on the farm and helped pay the mortgage, stifled his ambition in order that the favorite brother might be sent to college, and thereby scored a much greater success than the one for whom the sacrifice was made.

The girl who smothered her longings for a higher education or sacrificed the prospects of marriage and a home of her own, in order to take care of her aged parents, and was not known outside of her little coterie of friends, may have her name recorded far higher on the honor roll than that of the sister who went to college, or became a great author, musician, artist or actress.

In imperishable characters there will be inscribed on the success roll of honor names unfamiliar to most of us, the names of those who nobly performed humble parts in life; the unknown workers for humanity, the heroic sufferers,—some blind, some crippled or handicapped by the loss of hands or feet, or tortured by incurable diseases,—who, with a fortitude equal to that of the martyrs of old, took up life's burdens and bravely made the most of the powers and opportunities bestowed upon them by the Almighty.

***

CHAPTER IX
WHY DON'T YOU BEGIN?

When do you expect to do the wonderful things you have been dreaming about? Why don't you begin? What are you waiting for? Why don't you start? Are you waiting for a "good thing" to come to you, waiting for influence, for pull, for some one to help you?

Do you know that nothing is more demoralizing to the life, weakening to the character, than to be constantly wishing and dreaming of the great things we are going to do without a corresponding effort to actualize our dreams? Wishing without a corresponding effort to realize degenerates the mind, destroys initiative.

How many people deceive themselves into thinking that if they keep aspiring, if they keep longing to carry out their ideals, to reach their ambition, they will, without any other effort, actually realize their dreams! They do not seem to know that there is such a thing as aspiring too much, as forming the dreaming habit to one's injury.

Our visions are the plans of the possible life structure; but they will end merely in plans if we do not persistently follow them up with a vigorous effort to make them real; just as the architect's plans will end in his drawings if they are not followed up and made real by the builder.

Three things we must do to make our dreams come true. Visualize our desire. Concentrate on our vision. Work to bring it into the actual. The implements necessary for this are inside of us, not outside. No matter what the accidents of birth or fortune, there is only one force by which we can fashion our life material—mind.

All men who have achieved great things have been dreamers, and what they have accomplished has been just in proportion to the vividness, the energy and persistency with which they visualized their ideals; held to their dreams and struggled to make them come true.

"The crying evil of the young man who enters the business world to-day is the lack of application, preparation, thoroughness, with ambition but without the willingness to struggle to gain his desired end," says Theodore N. Vail.

It is one thing to have the ability and the desire to do something distinctive, something individual, but doing it is a very different thing. There is a tremendous amount of unproductive ability in the great failure army to-day. Why didn't the men who have it make something of themselves? Many of those men could be prosperous, successful men of standing in their community, instead of mendicants in a bread line. They had the opportunity to make good. Why didn't they?

It is a good thing to ask ourselves every now and then whether we are making good; whether we are making the most of our opportunities; whether we are going up or down. Oliver Wendel Holmes says it does not matter so much where we stand as the direction in which we are moving.

In what direction are you moving?

There are thousands of people in this country to-day who have splendid ambitions, who have made resolutions to carry out those ambitions, but who are cowering victims of doubt, which keeps them from making a start. They are just waiting. They are unable to make a beginning while this monster stands at the door of their resolution. They are afraid to burn their bridges behind them, to commit themselves to their purpose.

At the very outset of your career it is a splendid thing to make up your mind that you are going to be a conqueror in life, that you are going to be the king of your mental realm and not a slave to any treacherous enemy; that you will choose the wisest course, and, no matter how forbidding or formidable the difficulties in the way, that you will take the turning which points toward the goal of your ambition, no matter who or what may bar your onward path. Don't let doubt balk your efforts. Don't let it paralyze your beginning and make you a pigmy so that you will not half try to make good when you have a waiting giant in you. Confidence, self-assurance, self-faith—these are the great friends which will kill the traitor doubt.

The fact that you have an almost uncontrollable impulse, a great absorbing ambition to do a thing which meets with the approval of your judgment and your better self, is a notice served upon you that you can do the thing, and should do it at once.

Do not be afraid of taking responsibilities. Make up your mind that you will assume any responsibility which comes to you along the line of your legitimate career and that you will bear it a little better than anybody else ever before has. There is no greater mistake in the world than that of postponing present responsibility thinking that we will be better prepared to assume it later. It is accepting these positions as they come to us that gives us the preparation; for we can do nothing of importance easily, effectively, until we have done it so many times that it becomes a habit.

How often we hear people make remarks like this: "I know that I ought to do this thing to-day, but I do not believe I will," or "I do not feel like it." So they, perhaps, procrastinate, or let the thing slide along, and do just the opposite to what they know they ought to do.

If those who are disappointed with what they have so far accomplished, would only make up their minds that for one month they would force themselves to do the things they dislike, but which they know would be for their good, they would get a new start on the success road, a grip on themselves and their possibilities. Their whole work system would feel the resultant tonic.

On the very resolution to do the thing which is best for you—no matter how disagreeable, no matter how humiliating, no matter how much you may suffer from sensitiveness or a feeling of unpreparedness—depends the development of your manhood, or womanhood.

Why be afraid to demand great things of yourself? Affirm your ability to do and be and powers which you never dreamed you possessed will leap to your assistance. "Trust thyself. Every heart vibrates to that iron string."

There is no one that can shut the door which leads to any legitimate ambition, to a larger, fuller life, but yourself. There are no obstacles, no difficulties, no power on earth, nothing but yourself that can make God's promise to man void: "Behold, I have set before you an open door which no man can shut."

We are all reservoirs of power, and what we make of ourselves, what we achieve in life, is not dependent on the outward things, but on the extent to which we draw on our hidden forces, our latent talents and resources.

Whatever comes to us in life we create first in our mentality. As the building is a reality in all its details in the architect's mind before a stone or brick is laid, so we create mentally everything which later becomes a reality in our achievement. Our heart longings, our soul aspirations, are something more than mere vaporings of imagination. They are prophecies, predictions, couriers, forerunners of things that can become realities.

Hold the picture, the plan of the man or woman you long to be and that you are resolved to be, and stick to your mental plan of a glorious future. Do not give up in your discouraged moments or allow any obstacle to blur your ideals. Persist in visualizing the ideal man you are determined to be, and always think of yourself as you are ambitious to become. This mental attitude will help you to match your dream with its reality. There is a magnetic, attractive power in such a mighty purpose, in clinging to one unwavering aim. This sort of mental attitude and effort will establish your relation between yourself and the thing you are seeking.

THE END

www.ingramcontent.com/pod-product-compliance
Lightning Source LLC
LaVergne TN
LVHW101933220826
846093LV00009B/442